Three Little Rabbits Go Visiting

Pictures by

Marie H. Henry

Story by Ruth McCarthy

HEINEMANN : LONDON

William Heinemann Ltd
10 Upper Grosvenor Street, London W1X 9PA
LONDON MELBOURNE TORONTO
JOHANNESBURG AUCKLAND

First published 1985

Originally published in French by éditions Duculot,
Paris-Gembloux (1985).
434 94334 7
Printed in Belgium by Offset Printing Van den Bossche.
Photolitho by E. Beverari, Verona

For Bénédicte

One day the postman brought
a letter for Mama Rabbit
inviting the three little rabbits
to spend the day with
Aunt Flora.

I wonder if they'll be good today,
thought Mama Rabbit.

She stood outside the boys' bedroom
and heard some *very* loud noises —

but when she opened the door, she couldn't see anybody!

'Now calm down, children,' said Mama Rabbit. 'You're going to Aunt Flora's for the day.'

'Oh quick, let's get dressed,' said Libby, dashing into her own bedroom.

Loppy and Hoppy thought it would be fun to help Mama first, so they climbed up and took down her best hat from the wardrobe.

Mama Rabbit thought it looked lovely ... but the naughty little rabbits had a different idea.

They decided to cut
off the big feather.

Mama *was* upset.

'Don't worry, Mama,' said Libby,
'this flower will look much prettier than
the feather.'

'Hurry, hurry,' shouted Hoppy,
'it's already ten o'clock.'

Loppy and Hoppy rushed to their room, put on their best jackets and tied their bows.

Hoppy's wasn't very good.

Libby tied her bow too.

Then Mama said, ‘Come along everyone, we really must go now. Aunt Flora and your cousins will be waiting for us.’

So they set off through the woods to Aunt Flora's house.

Aunt Flora hugged the three little rabbits,
then took them out to play with their cousins.

They played all kinds of games together.

After they'd had a rest Libby said,
'I know what we can do —
we can play croquet!'

So they set out all the
hoops, and everyone
took a mallet,

and they hit the balls through the hoops until their cousin Timmy hit Libby's ball right out of the game, and she was *furious*.

What a bad rabbit she was!

She hit poor Timmy
so hard he had to have
two bandages.

Then she was sorry, and they
kissed and hugged and
made friends again.

At teatime they all sat down in the garden together and Aunt Flora gave them an enormous cherry cake and lots and lots of orange juice.

After tea everyone wanted a story, so Libby fetched a big book down from the shelf, and Loppy carried it to Aunt Flora.

Then all the little rabbits sat quietly while Aunt Flora read to them.

When it was time to go home
the whole family stood at the gate and
waved goodbye.

The three little rabbits were all so tired that by the time they reached their house they were fast asleep. So Mama Rabbit put them straight to bed.

Good night.